THE Oyster Garden

Camille Klump

DEDICATION:

I would like to thank the city of Oldsmar, Florida, for their support throughout this project. With special mention to Mayor Dan Saracki and Mr. Eric Seidel. I am also grateful to my artist Mike Roberts, who generously gave of his creativity because he believed in getting this green message out to kids everywhere. Whenever I write about the beauty of this planet, I remember my grandmother Julia; the first person to introduce me to the value of a green world.

Teaching and encouraging little ones to go green can be a daunting task for any parent or teacher, and finding a project which holds their attention, captures their imagination, and gets them out in the field, well - that in itself, is another challenge. But the city of Oldsmar in Upper Tampa Bay, Florida, has managed to do exactly that.

They conducted a one-hour workshop which gave participants an opportunity to meet members in their community, local officials, environmental scientists, and other volunteers. Attendees learned how valuable oysters were in helping to filter and purify polluted water, and they were educated on how vertical hanging oyster gardens and artificial oyster reefs beds were being used across the US and around the world, to help restore damaged shorelines, bays, and oceans. In this interactive workshop, participants were taught to measure and cut lengths of rope and thread half of a recycled oyster shell through it. The city demonstrated how to drill holes and insert screws in the side of a pier, to hang the oyster gardens. Everyone was invited to take their vertical oyster gardens home with them, to install on their own docks.

Parents were encouraged to bring their kids back to revisit the project site at four months intervals to help monitor and record the progress of the garden, as well as test the water to see how effective the oysters were in removing pollutants. The concept of using vertical hanging oyster gardens and artificial oyster reefs, extends from Tampa Bay to Chesapeake Bay and to other parts of the United States. Other countries around the world, like the U.K. and Australia, have also used these methods with remarkable success.

This in- the- field green project is fun, engaging, and educational. It is perfect for your little junior scientist, aspiring environmentalist, or even if you simply want to teach your little ones how they can help fight climate change. I am sure you will find conservation projects like this and many others, in your own community. After all, wouldn't you like to leave the next generation a planet where the air is clean, the waters are pure and natural resources are abundant?

Camille Klump

Other climate change books by the author include:
A Simple Seagrass
A Code Red Christmas and
A Message from Santa

There once were sparkling oceans and
beautiful crystal-clear bays,

Where coasts were kissed by sunshine,
the warm air salty from ocean spray.

But over time the water's changed— it's dirty now, and smelly.

Pesticides, junk, and garbage are now lodged inside its belly.

Toxic red tide grows, spreads, and gets worse every year.

It's poisoning all our sea life and harming humans, too, I fear.

Candy wrappers, bottles, and tins, all the stuff
that belong in our bins,

Plastic straws, fishing line, and more of our
junk that gets left behind.

Fertilizer in your garden that
helps your flowers grow

With heavy rains will wash
away and into the ocean flow.

They sweep into the ocean,
hurting every living thing.

Environmental disaster is what this
litter soon will bring.

But vertical hanging oyster gardens
can surely change all that—
I'm pretty sure you didn't know baby
oysters are known as spat.

Oysters pump and filter water through
gills just like a fish,
The very same half shell oysters that's
served upon a dish.

My city teaches kids like me to string oyster shells on a rope.

Our mayor says that living gardens will give our oceans hope!

So, after you eat and leave your seat, the shells
are not thrown away.

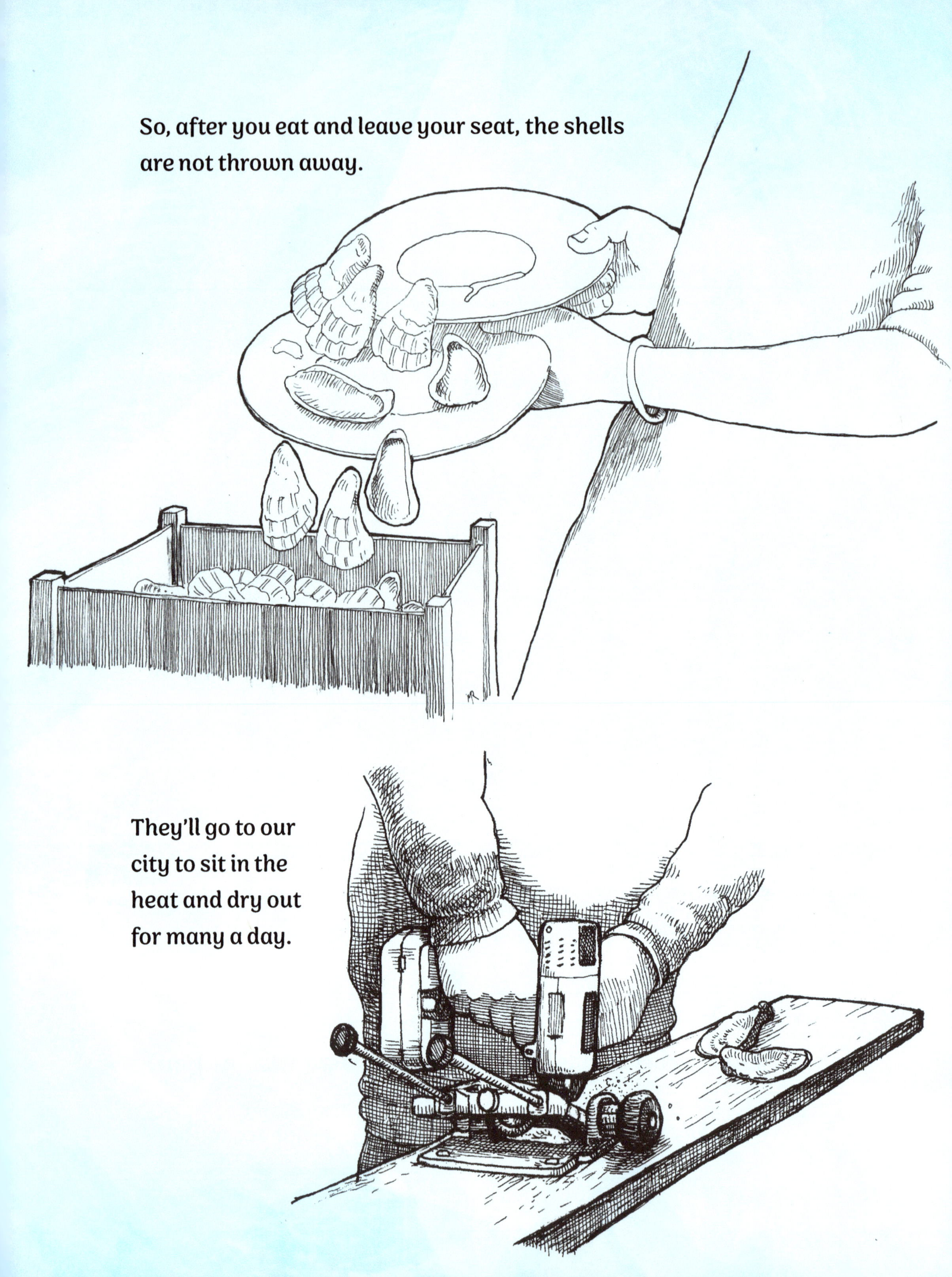

They'll go to our
city to sit in the
heat and dry out
for many a day.

We'll put our shells on three feet of rope, that will last through sun and rain

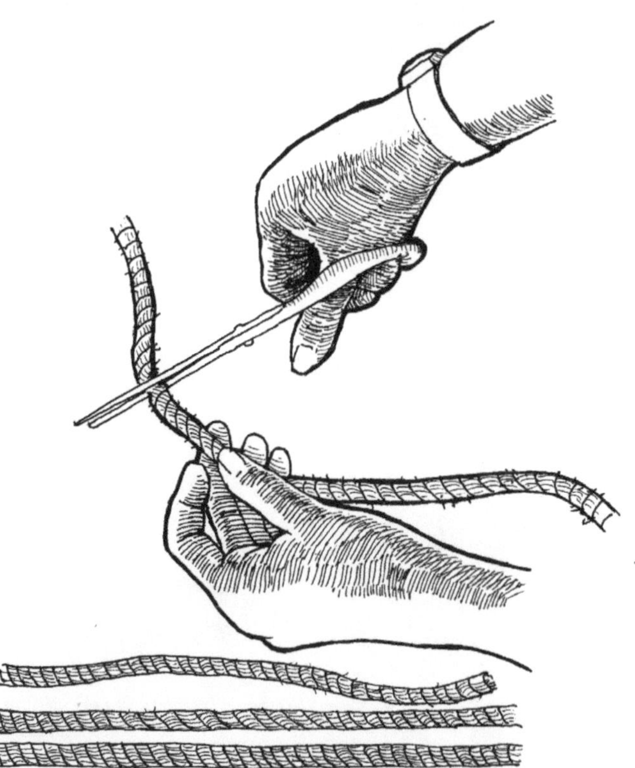

By threading the rope through a hole in half shell, it's like stringing beads on a chain.

With thirty shells strung on the rope,
soon to hang from your dock

In time to form a concrete glue, one that
will be stronger than a rock!

But first you'll need some help to drill, a screw in the
side of your dock,

A place to tie your little oyster garden. Now gently let it drop.

Several more screws on the sides of
the dock, spaced several feet apart,

Are all it takes from you and I, to
give our baby oysters a start.

In several months, the little spat will attach and begin to grow.

They'll start to filter water in the bay — it's clever don't you know.

But always remember to keep in mind that tides will come and go:

A lesson you'll find, as the garden hides, if it's been hung too high
or too low.

Can that be it, such a simple solution, to help restore our bay?
An oyster garden that fights pollution-cleans fifty gallons of water a day!

In time the knot on the rope will rot, and the garden will fall to the floor.

And here in the Bay, an oyster bed will stay, a home for crabs, fish and more.

I hope that kids will one day say, they left
their world so much greener,

They learned to use living oyster gardens,
to make the oceans so much cleaner.

The City of Oldsmar is dedicated to protecting our environment. 30% of our area is devoted to parks and preserves. Oldsmar is located at the top of Tampa Bay in the state of Florida. Our three parks are situated on our shoreline – the Mobbly Bayou Wilderness Preserve and Beach Park, Veteran's Memorial Park, and R.E. Olds Park. They are treasures within Oldsmar. Every day they are gathering places for children, families, and all types of community events. You can enjoy picnics and nature trails, watch the amazing sunsets, fish off the pier, and see the manatees swim slowly by. My grandsons love chasing squirrels and seeing crabs on the shoreline. R.E. Olds Park was where our oyster garden project- the mayor's challenge was launched.

Pollution and human activity are slowly destroying our precious ecosystems therefore we must work together to protect the waters, mangroves, and wetlands of Tampa Bay. We must continue to improve the quality of the water, improve flow to increase oxygen to the waterway, bring back the oyster beds and restore the lost habitat of the shoreline.

Old Tampa Bay deserves to be preserved for generations to come and there are many conservation projects that children can volunteer for. We must all do whatever we can to keep our beautiful planet healthy forever.

Dan Saracki
Mayor
City of Oldsmar, FL

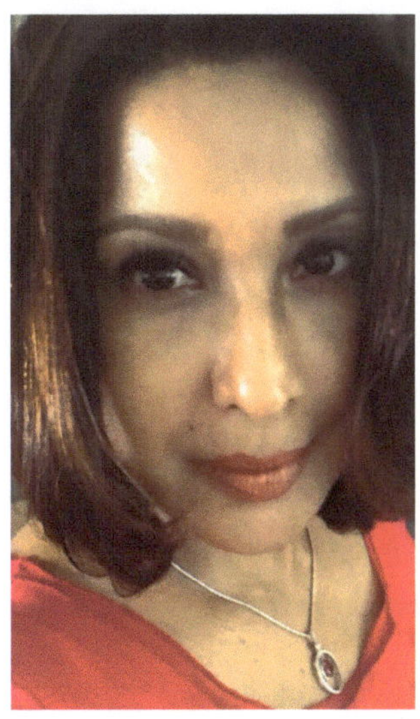

Passionate about nature, Camille Klump is an advocate for conservation in the Tampa Bay Area and the Amazon rainforest. She has written several books which help children understand the importance of protecting the planet. Some of her stories revolve around community environmental projects, as a way to encourage children to experience the positive effects of going green. The city of Oldsmar, as well as Tampa Bay Watch, have recognized her contribution in highlighting the value, beauty, and fragility of Florida's diverse ecosystems, through her children's books.

Camille has written six books and is set to release a seventh.